# Windmills

Published in 2026 by
**Norwood House Press**
2544 Clinton Street
Buffalo, NY 14224



Printed in the United States of America

Library of Congress Cataloging-in-Publication Data:
Names: Atkins, Jill (Children's author). | Rickard, Stephen, 1957-, author. | Rix, Nicolas, illustrator.
Title: Windmills / written by Jill Atkins. Butter brains / written by Stephen Rickard, illustrated by Nicolas Rix.
Description: Buffalo, NY : Norwood House Press, 2026. | Series: Phonics all-stars: phase 4 |
Identifiers: ISBN 9781978578807 (pbk.) | ISBN 9781978578814 (library bound) | ISBN 9781978578821 (ebook)
Subjects: LCSH: Reading–Phonetic method–Juvenile fiction. | English language–Phonetics–Juvenile fiction. | Wind turbines–Juvenile fiction. | Wind power–Juvenile fiction. | Superheroes–Juvenile fiction. | Extraterrestrial beings–Juvenile fiction.
Classification: LCC LB1573.3 A796 2026 | DDC 372.465–dc23

CPSIA compliance information: Batch #CW26NHP: For further information contact Norwood House Press at 1-800-237-9932.

Windmills have sails.

Look at some of the odd sails you might see on a windmill.

Gusts of wind turn the sails.

The sails turn cogs in the windmill.

Cogs are terrific tools. See how they all connect up in the windmill.

Then they all turn as one big tool.

Can you see the big flat discs of hard rock? They are crushing corn seeds as they turn.

The corn seeds turn to powder.

The miller fills sacks with the powder from the corn seeds.

Then the miller sells the sacks for cooking.

This is not a windmill, but it is still a mill.

It has cogs too, but it needs a gushing river to turn the cogs.

Its discs crush the corn seeds, just like in the windmill.

Some windmills pump liquid out from flat land.

Some windmills pump liquid up from deep down under the soil.

This is good for the sheep and the crops.

This is a wind farm.

You might see hundreds of windmills.

Some are inland. Some are off the coast.

This is a big windmill!

We get power from this sort of windmill.

We get light from that power – and we can cook with it too.

We need windmills!

# Butter Brains

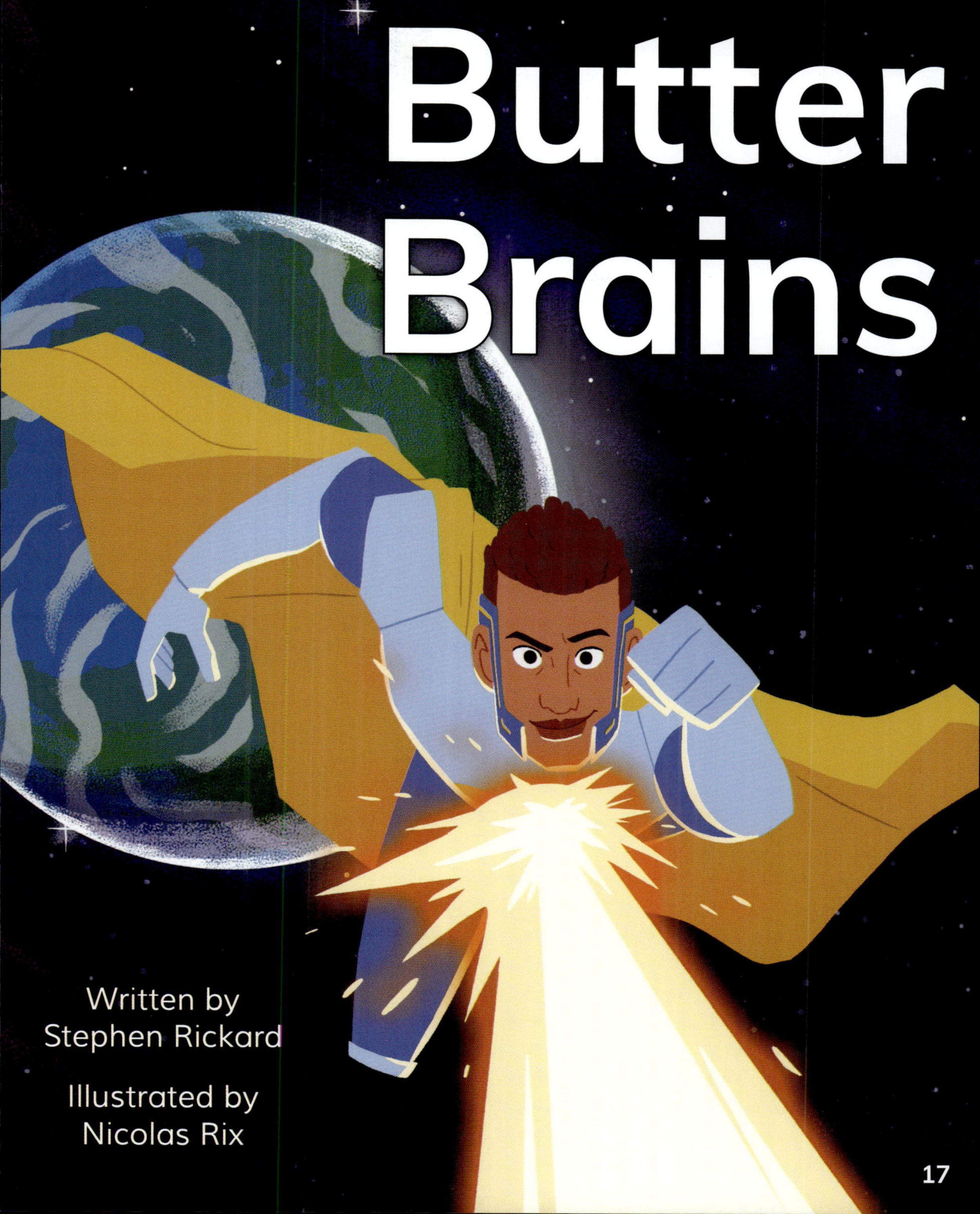

Written by
Stephen Rickard

Illustrated by
Nicolas Rix

On a ship far, far off ...
Stand up! Now coil up this red cord and twist the end.
Then fix it to the box.

This is such a good plan. I think this will be the best stunt ever.

In a wet town, on the coast, Tim is on the job.
Quick, hop to it! We need to speed off with all this loot.
LOOT

Trust me. I can fix this.

Bad luck, Tim!
Bang!

Ow!
I cannot hear
a thing. My ears
are ringing.

Back on the ship ...
Point that thing at the target. Grab it tight and aim it.
Now press the power ... and off we go!
This melts brains as if they are butter. I cannot wait to see it start.

Beep!
Beep!
ZZAP!

The "beep, beep" thing hits its target.
Look! This cannot be good!
My ears! The racket is too much!

Then ...

Such a lot of blank looks!

It looks as if that "beep, beep" thing might not be nonsense.

Look at Tim! His brains are not butter.

This is bad. I think I need to fix it.

Will Tim fix it? Can we trust him?

It looks like we can!
ZIP!

Good job, Tim. My brain is back.
You set us all free!
Are you chatting to me? I cannot hear a thing!

ICONS

# BEYONCÉ

BY BETH GOTTLIEB

Enslow PUBLISHING

**Please visit our website, www.enslow.com.**
**For a free color catalog of all our high-quality books, call toll free 1-800-398-2504 or fax 1-877-980-4454.**

**Library of Congress Cataloging-in-Publication Data**

Names: Gottlieb, Beth, author.
Title: Beyoncé / Beth Gottlieb.
Description: Buffalo, NY : Enslow Publishing, 2025. | Series: Icons | Includes index.
Identifiers: LCCN 2023056552 | ISBN 9781978540071 (library binding) | ISBN 9781978540064 (paperback) | ISBN 9781978540088 (ebook)
Subjects: LCSH: Beyoncé, 1981–Juvenile literature. | Singers–United States–Biography–Juvenile literature.
Classification: LCC ML3930.K66 G67 2025 | DDC 782.42164092 [B]–dc23/eng/20231212
LC record available at https://lccn.loc.gov/2023056552

Portions of this work were originally authored by Michou Kennon and published as *Beyoncé*. All new material in this edition is authored by Beth Gottlieb.

Published in 2025 by
**Enslow Publishing**
2544 Clinton Street
Buffalo, NY 14224



Designer: Tanya Dellaccio Keeney
Editor: Kristen Rajczak Nelson

Photo credits: Cover DFree/Shutterstock.com; p. 5 Image Press Agency/Alamy.com; p. 7 UPI/Alamy.com; p. 9 Featureflash Photo Agency/Shutterstock.com; p. 11 Everett Collection/Shutterstock.com; pp. 13, 21 WENN Rights Ltd/Alamy.com; p. 15 ZUMA Press, Inc./Alamy.com; p. 17 Abaca Press/Alamy.com; p. 19 Shakeyjon/Alamy.com; pp. 23, 25 Album/Alamy.com; p. 26 Jeff Bukowski/Shutterstock.com; p. 27 https://upload.wikimedia.org/wikipedia/commons/6/60/Beyoncé_-_Tottenham_Hotspur_Stadium_-_1st_June_2023_(47_of_118)_(52946286530)_(cropped).jpg; p. 29 https://upload.wikimedia.org/wikipedia/commons/b/b7/Beyoncé_-_Tottenham_Hotspur_Stadium_-_1st_June_2023_(10_of_118)_(52946364598)_(best_crop).jpg.



Printed in the United States of America

CPSIA compliance information: Batch #CSENS25: For further information contact Enslow Publishing at 1-800-398-2504.

# Contents



Words in the glossary appear in **bold** the first time they are used in the text.

# Ultimate Icon

Beyoncé is a Renaissance woman. She's not only a singer and **performer**, but also a mother, a businesswoman, and a director. Her hard work has led to a level of success almost no one today can match. She truly is an **icon**!

## ICONIC!

*Beyoncé told GQ magazine in 2013: "I now know that, yes, I am powerful."*

# Early On

Beyoncé Giselle Knowles was born on September 4, 1981. She grew up in Houston, Texas. Beyoncé began performing when she was just 7 years old. She won over 30 singing and dancing contests! By age 10, she had started recording music.

Solange

## ICONIC!

*Beyoncé has a sister named Solange. She's a well-known singer too!*

In 1990, Beyoncé and some friends formed a singing group called Girls Tyme. They were later called Destiny's Child. The first Destiny's Child **album** came out in 1998. The group had many hit songs and won two Grammy **Awards**!

## ICONIC!

***Beyoncé wrote parts of some of the best-known Destiny's Child songs, including "Say My Name" and "Survivor."***

Destiny's Child

# On Her Own

Beyoncé made an album on her own called *Dangerously in Love* that came out in 2003. Its hit song "Crazy in Love" featured rapper JAY-Z. She won five Grammy Awards, including best R&B song. In 2004, the last Destiny's Child album came out. Then the group broke up.

## ICONIC!

*Beyoncé has appeared in the movies* The Pink Panther, Cadillac Records, Dreamgirls, *and more.*

Beyoncé's second album was called *B'Day*. It came out in the United States the day after her birthday in 2006. Beyoncé's 2008 album was called *I Am . . . Sasha Fierce*. She called herself "Sasha Fierce" to feel brave on stage.

**ICONIC!**

*In 2008, Beyoncé and JAY-Z got married!*

# Hitmaker

At the Grammy Awards in 2010, Beyoncé won more Grammys than any other woman has won in one night ever! She won six. Her song "Single Ladies (Put a Ring on It)" won song of the year! The following year, Beyoncé put out another album called *4*.

## ICONIC!

*Beyoncé and JAY-Z had their first daughter in 2012, Blue Ivy Carter. In 2017, they also had twins, Rumi and Sir.*

Beyoncé performed the halftime show at the Super Bowl in 2013. She brought out members of Destiny's Child too. More than 110 million people watched it! Later that year, she surprised fans with the album *Beyoncé*.

## ICONIC!

*Beyoncé founded BeyGOOD in 2013. The* ***charity*** *has helped people around the world, including those harmed by big storms, kids in need of school supplies, and Black-owned businesses.*

# Getting Personal

In 2016, Beyoncé put out another surprise album called *Lemonade*. It came out after the first airing of a short film also called *Lemonade*. The album had very personal **lyrics**. It included appearances from other music artists including Kendrick Lamar and the Weeknd.

## ICONIC!

*Beyoncé owns her own company, Parkwood Entertainment. She also owns the fashion line IVY PARK.*

# Top Billing

*Everything Is Love*, a **collaboration** between JAY-Z and Beyoncé under the name The Carters, came out in 2018. They won a Grammy for their work! That year Beyoncé became the first Black woman to headline the music **festival** Coachella in California.

## ICONIC!

*To headline a festival means an artist is the top performer (or one of the top performers) at a festival. Beyoncé also headlined the Glastonbury Festival in England in 2011.*

In 2019, a movie following Beyoncé as she got ready for Coachella came out. It showed her performance too. It was called *Homecoming: A Film by Beyoncé*. She also put out a live album. Beyoncé was the voice of Nala in *The Lion King* in 2019 too!

## ICONIC!

*Beyoncé was one of the directors of* Homecoming. *She also directed the* ***visual album*** Black Is King *that came out in 2020.*

# Setting Records

Beyoncé won four Grammys in 2021, including best R&B song for her song "Black Parade." She now had 28 Grammy Awards. She set the record for most Grammy wins for a female artist!

## ICONIC!

*"Black Parade" came out on Juneteenth, the holiday celebrating when the last enslaved people in the United States were freed. It showed support for Black people in the United States.*

In 2022, Beyoncé's long-awaited album came out. It was called *act i: Renaissance*. She won four more Grammy Awards. Now with 32 Grammy wins, Beyoncé had the most of any music artist, male or female, in history!

**ICONIC!**

*Beyoncé doesn't give a lot of interviews. She tries to keep her personal life private and shares only what she wants to.*

# Into the Future

In 2023, the concert film *Renaissance: A Film by Beyoncé* made more than $20 million in its opening weekend! It was filmed on Beyoncé's Renaissance Tour. The following year, Beyoncé announced a new album: *act ii: Cowboy Carter*. It would be her first country music album!

Renaissance concert movie poster

## ICONIC!

*In 2021, Beyoncé said: "I have paid my dues and followed every rule for decades, so now I can break the rules that need to be broken. My wish for the future is to continue to do everything everyone thinks I can't do."*

# Timeline

| | |
|---|---|
| 1981 | *Beyoncé is born on September 4 in Houston, Texas.* |
| 1998 | *Destiny's Child comes out with their first album.* |
| 2003 | *Beyoncé's first album becomes a hit.* |
| 2006 | B'Day *comes out.* |
| 2008 | I Am . . . Sasha Fierce *comes out.* |
| 2011 | 4 *comes out.* |
| 2013 | *Beyoncé performs the halftime show at the Super Bowl.* |
| 2016 | Lemonade *is released.* |
| 2018 | Everything Is Love *by The Carters comes out.* |
| 2019 | Homecoming *the live album and film come out.* |
| 2022 | act I: Renaissance *comes out.* |
| 2023 | Renaissance: A Film by Beyoncé *comes out. Beyoncé sets the record for most Grammy wins for any artist.* |
| 2024 | *Beyoncé releases her first country album.* |

# For More Information

## BOOKS

Daniels, Rachel. *Meet Beyoncé*. Hallandale, FL: Mitchell Lane Publishers, 2024.

Schuh, Mari C. *What You Never Knew About Beyoncé.* North Mankato, MN: Spark, an imprint of Capstone, 2023.

## WEBSITES

**BeyGOOD**
*https://beygood.org/*
Find out how Beyoncé gives back with her charity work. See how you can help too!

**Beyoncé Official Website**
*www.beyonce.com*
Keep up with Beyoncé's music and tours here.

**Publisher's note to educators and parents:** Our editors have carefully reviewed these websites to ensure that they are suitable for students. Many websites change frequently, however, and we cannot guarantee that a site's future contents will continue to meet our high standards of quality and educational value. Be advised that students should be closely supervised whenever they access the internet.

# Glossary

**album:** A musical recording that includes a set of certain songs.

**award:** A prize given for doing something.

**charity:** A group that helps people or animals in need.

**collaboration:** A work created with another person or people.

**festival:** A series of organized performances over a period of time.

**icon:** A person who is very successful and admired.

**lyrics:** The words of a song.

**performer:** One who performs, or plays music, dances, or sings.

**visual album:** A music album that has an accompanying film or music videos for each song.

# Index